Neighbou:

edited by

Harry Chambers & Chris Faram

PETERLOO POETS
in association with BBC English by Radio

First published in 1988
by Peterloo Poets
2 Kelly Gardens · Calstock · Cornwall PL18 9SA
Printed in Great Britain by
Latimer Trend & Company Ltd, Plymouth
All rights reserved

ISBN 1 871471 00 1

ACKNOWLEDGEMENTS

WITH THE ASSISTANCE OF

SOUTH WEST ARTS

Contents

interviews by Chris Faram (BBC English by Radio)

Dear

I and all the listeners to BBC English on the
World Service would be delighted if you would
write a short poem on the theme of
"Neighbours". I think that this subject will
give some idea of how we live in Britain, and
how we see ourselves (and those next door!)

As soon as I have received your poem, I will
be round to ask you some questions about the
language and references and what inspired you
to write what you did.

Please let me know what you think of this
idea.

Yours sincerely.

Chris

(Chris Faram)
Programme Organiser
BBC ENGLISH

Anna Adams

PASTORAL

Our neighbours are shepherds; our tousled croft
floats on their smooth green acres like a raft
manned by off-comed'uns, town comedians,
our cottage being an ark of art and craft.

Their byres are arks of cattle, bearing them
across white Winter; barns are arks of grass
that bear lofts full of fodder through the storm,
keeping sweet Summer dry in deluge-time.

Our croft has pastured children, bantam hens,
a tortoise, Chinese geese, stray tents, wild bees,
while their well-tended fields keep distant towns
in milk and mutton. We plant useless trees.

Yet we have more than drystone boundaries
in common; whirling years of suns and moons
have stolen youth and brought indignities;
we laugh a lot, hobnobbing in the lanes.

The sheep are neighbours too, with laundered fleeces
dyed pink and green, like punks, the whole flock races
across blue-shadowed snow to meet the tractor
distributing hay beards to hungry faces.

In lambing time our wastrels' croft grows green
as any other patch of April's quilt;
we lend it, free, to ewes that suckle twins;
at Christmas, Harry pays us with Old Malt.

Yes, we would weep, if opportunity
allowed, at one another's funerals:
meanwhile I praise the serendipity
that built a friendship through dividing walls.

INTERVIEW/ANNA ADAMS

This place as described in the poem really has a concrete feel to it. Is it a place that's very close to you?

It certainly is a real place. It's in Upper Ribblesdale in North Yorkshire where we have lived for quite a long time, like 30 years, on and off.

There's a feeling, specific references in the poem, to you being different from the other people.

Well, farmers are farmers and artists are artists, and town people look on nature as being benevolent. Country people know you have to work terribly hard to get anything out of it.

You're quite self-critical in this poem. Your choice of words suggests that you feel the difference between yourselves and your productive neighbours.

We're very productive too, but poems have very little cash value. I wanted to write a sort of reassuring, basic poem about the sort of things that life is founded on, which is not supermarkets or buses in the street.

Let's look at the language. Why do you see yourselves as "comedians"?

They see us as comedians, or did.

"The sheep are neighbours too, with laundered fleeces/dyed pink and green."
Why are the sheep dyed?

They're washed several times a year to keep ticks and things out, and they're dyed pink and green to indicate who they belong to. Different farmers have different colours and different distribution: two blue dots or one red and one blue.

What about "the tractor/distributing hay beards"?

Well, a lot of sheep munching hay, they don't get it all in their mouths at once; it dangles down, making them look like a lot of bearded ladies.

Do you feel, looking at the poem as a whole, that this refers to an optimistic period in your life, or do you feel that because you refer to "dividing walls", "useless trees", etc., that there was a division between you and your neighbours?

Well, naturally there is a division. We came from something totally different, from London, to live there. And artists are always rather misfits anywhere. But we were very lucky in our neighbours. Country people are very different from town people. I don't think it ever occurred to me that anybody might not like us really. You are aware of a difference: for instance, when we first got there, somebody said, "We hear that you're artists and we've been that worried about you, however are you going to earn a living up here? None of us can afford to have our portraits painted." There's such a thing as landscape, there's such a thing as imaginative art, and there's such a thing as the art market in London or in cities. But it was a world that they were all totally unaware of. Then there was something on the news about some Reynolds or other famous pictures having been stolen in an art robbery, and the local policeman came round and asked us questions about it, and looked from side to side to see if he could see any Reynolds's leaning against the wall anywhere.

Can you tell me about how, when you were asked to write about the theme of "Neighbours", what inspired you, how you started?

First of all I was rather worried, because I thought I ought to write something of international import about the third world or hunger or something—all men are brothers and all the rest of it—which I firmly believe. But then I thought I have to write about the world I know and carry on writing about sheep and shepherds and direct experience.

GLOSSARY
"tousled croft" (line 1): a neglected piece of land, probably full of nettles and thistles.
"off-comed'uns" (line 3): a local word for people who come from (far)-off.
"fodder" (line 7): hay—stored to feed cows in the winter.
"deluge-time" (line 8): this place has a regular rainy season. "Deluge" conjures up images of the Ark and Noah and the Biblical Flood.
"drystone boundaries" (line 13): walls made of large pieces of stone that are fitted together without using mortar.
"hobnobbing" (line 16): chatting, friendly exchange of gossip.
"wastrels'" (line 21): belonging to people who are neglectful, let things go to waste.
"quilt" (line 22): the fields fit together in rectangular patterns like those on a patchwork quilt bedcover.
"ewes" (line 23): female sheep.
"serendipity" (line 27): happy chance; happy, accidental discovery.

photo by Marti Friedlander

Fleur Adcock

14

NEXT DOOR

You could have called it the year of their persecution:
some villain robbed her window-boxes of half
her petunias and pansies. She wrote a notice:
"To the person who took my plants. I am disabled;
they cost me much labour to raise from seed."
Next week, the rest went. Then his number-plates:
not the car itself. (Who'd want the car? It stank.)
A gale blew in a pane of their front window—
crack: just like that! Why theirs? Why not, for example,
mine? Same gale; same row of elderly houses.

And through it all, the cats multiplied fatly—
fatly but scruffily (his weak heart, her illness:
"They need grooming, I know, but they're fat as butter")
—and the fleas hopped, and the smell came through the walls.
How many cats? Two dozen? Forty? Fifty?
We could count the ones outside in the cages (twelve),
but inside? Always a different furry face
at a window; and the kittens—think of the kittens
pullulating like maggots over the chairs!
Someone reported them to the authorities.

Who could have done it? Surely not a neighbour!
"No, not a neighbour! Someone in the Fancy"—
she was certain. "They've always envied my success.
The neighbours wouldn't . . ." A sunny afternoon;
I aimed my camera at them over the fence,
at their garden table, under the striped umbrella:
"Smile!" And they grinned: his gnome-hat, her witch-hair
in the sun—well out of earshot of the door-bell
and of the Environmental Health Inspector.
You could call it a bad year. But the next was worse.

INTERVIEW/FLEUR ADCOCK

Is this a true story? Are the events here as they happened?

They were people I knew for many years who lived next door to me—
they're both dead now. Their lives gradually went downhill—they
weren't well, and they had all these cats, and not as much money as they
needed for the cats. Then somehow fate turned against them.

You talk about them with a fair degree of humour. Was it always like this?

It was both appalling and touching. I felt terribly sorry for them. They
were entertaining in their weird way, but they were also suffering. Other
neighbours, if they read the poem, will probably laugh with recognition,
because we all went through this "what are we going to do about the
smell?", and yet we were all—all the ones I spoke to—were far too . . .
well, it would have upset us to think of reporting them. We wouldn't
have reported them, because the cats were the lifeblood of this rather
sad couple. So that now that fate's resolved it, we can laugh looking
back.

How did you actually shape your thoughts?

Well, what I was trying to do was compress the events of a number of
years into something like 30 lines. So I decided to concentrate on the last
year of the people's lives, and seized on this first line at some point: "You
could have called it the year of their persecution". And then a fairly
straightforward recital of some of the events. In fact it's in three
sections, and the first section has the particular persecution which was
taking place, things being stolen from them, or damaged. Then the
second section focuses on the cats. Then in the third section there's the
woman's delusions about her neighbours. She assumes that none of the
neighbours would wish to do her any damage—they couldn't have
stolen the plants or damaged the car, or reported her to the authorities.
So it must be someone in the cat-breeding fraternity, the Fancy, who's
resenting her because of her success. She won a number of prizes for her
cats. So it's the way she shelters herself from reality that occupies the last
section. And then suddenly reality slams in. I'm not specific about that,
but I think it could be guessed what the something worse was that was
going to happen.

16

In the second stanza who is speaking?

She's speaking. She is the one who says "They need grooming, I know, but they're fat as butter". She's apologising for the fact that they're rather untidy and bedraggled.

"Fat as butter" was said in a critical manner?

No: she's saying "they're fat as butter", meaning "I look after them, I make sure they don't go hungry".

When you say they were reported to the authorities, by "authorities" you mean?

I mean the Environmental Health Inspector. People complaining about the smell, and the actual or possible fleas, the fact that a house it was thought should have been restricted to domestic use was being used for cat breeding on a pretty large scale.

And the authorities responded and came round?

They came round, yes.

But the immediate neighbours, the subject of the poem, couldn't believe that it was a neighbour who'd reported them?

No, they felt sure that people who sympathised with them in all their misfortunes, as people did with their misfortunes about the plants and the car, didn't strike them as the people who would then go off and report them. I don't think anyone really knows who did, so it remains a mystery.

GLOSSARY
"pullulating" (line 19): not just wriggling, but swarming; a surging mass of kittens, climbing up over each other and falling down and getting tangled up.

Gillian Clarke

NEIGHBOURS

That spring was late. We watched the sky
and studied charts for shouldering isobars.
Birds were late to pair. Crows drank from the lamb's eye.

Over Finland small birds fell: song-thrushes
steering north, smudged signatures on light,
migrating warblers, nightingales.

Wing-beats failed over fjiords, each lung a sip of gall.
Children were warned of their dangerous beauty.
Milk was spilt in Poland. Each quarrel

the blowback from some old story,
a mouthful of bitter air from the Ukraine
brought by the wind out of its box of sorrows.

This spring a lamb sips caesium on a Welsh hill.
A child, lifting her head to drink the rain,
takes into her blood the poisoned arrow.

Now we are all neighbourly, each little town
in Europe twinned to Chernobyl, each heart
with the burnt firemen, the child on the Moscow train.

In the democracy of the virus and the toxin
we wait. We watch for spring migrations,
one bird returning with green in its voice.

Glasnost. Golau glas. A first break of blue.

INTERVIEW/GILLIAN CLARKE

Where do you live and what sort of neighbours do you have?

I live in hill country in the south-west part of Wales, and my neighbours are mainly sheep farmers.

What actually triggered your "Neighbours" poem?

The commission focused the poem I wanted to write about Chernobyl. But it's too easy to write a crass political poem, and it isn't at all intended to have one iota of politics in it. It's about the human race. My own area was not affected by Chernobyl, but Wales was affected, as indeed the north-west of England and Northern Ireland and Scotland were. Rainy areas, mountain areas. We, in fact, were lucky in our area—it didn't rain that day. But I think even if I'd lived in the south of England I would have felt touched. When you see children putting their heads up to lick rain—did you do that when you were a child? I certainly did; you opened your mouth and drank snow or rain—you suddenly realise that drop of rain could contain the leukaemia that they might get one day. It's just the most terrifying thought. But I was no sorrier for the child on a hill in Wales than for the child who I saw on the television being packed off from the town in Russia to Moscow, to stay with relations. So to me those two children were the key to the poem.

Did knowing that you were writing for radio listeners, who might never actually see the poem, affect you?

I read not only on radio, but I also read to audiences. I know as a listener to poetry that you need to have something to see, as well as something to hear, as well as something to think about afterwards. So I always put in something to see. That's where the "shouldering isobars" come from, by the way. It's the weather forecast, of course, on television, not radio. Most people, perhaps, if they understand the word "isobar" at all, would see what I mean when I say "shouldering". When the weather-man points them out, there they are, pushing other weather out of the way, pushing their long shoulders across the Atlantic towards us. The other thing is the birds, the migrating birds. They were actually taken from a newspaper report. The birds that they were worrying about were song-thrushes and nightingales and warblers: they were migrating and they were falling out of the sky in flocks. Therefore I put in a visual image, the "smudged signatures", which I hope is a bit like what you see when you look in the sky and see migrating birds.

Let's look at some of the expressions in the poem. Tell me about "each lung a sip of gall". Does "gall" have two meanings there?

Well, I mean it to be a bitter poison. The birds that were found had poison in their lungs, and I thought that rain was only a sip to a bird, but enough to fill a whole lung with poison. The poison, of course, that was given to Christ, in a way: gall.

Also, I believe, it's a growth on an oak apple, suggesting some malformation.

That's right. Malformation, yes, some horrible event in the body.

"Milk was spilt in Poland"—you mean deliberately?

They threw it away—they had to throw it all away. We in fact didn't throw it away, and perhaps we should have done. But in Poland they threw all the milk away. Milk is so innocent, it seemed to me to be an extraordinary thought.

The stanza beginning "Now we are all neighbourly, each little town/in Europe twinned to Chernobyl"—perhaps "twinned" has connotations for us that may not be obvious to others?

Yes, twin towns. I'm sure all the towns in Europe who have a twin with a town in Britain will understand that. Suddenly it seemed to me, thinking of all that business of twinning with towns in other parts of Europe in particular, but in some cases further afield, that suddenly our hearts were all with Chernobyl, we were all sympathetic towards what had happened there. Our hearts were in our boots. From here we can see the power station across the Bristol Channel, near Bristol, in Somerset. There it is, a white and shining castle, also a box of sorrows. Where could it happen? It could have happened anywhere in the world, perhaps, and our hearts were with them. So we are twinned, we feel close to those people.

GLOSSARY
"Glasnost" (line 22): openness. (Russian)
"Golau glas" (line 22): blue light, or open skies. (Welsh)

21

photo by Graham De Smidt

Fred D'Aguiar

FRONTLINE CHRONICLE

1.
Our differences loomed larger as Airships
A stone's throw high: "Whatever you say
Must be said direct, no embroidery,
No honeying the facts to make them palatable".
He pushed bodily from the table,
His weight grating the chair on the boards.
I was nailed there, my blood rising, feeling
A faint shudder I tried to fight worsen.

I shouted at the door, "You don't know."
As a girl granny saw her first blimp
Fill the sky and stoned it.
"What does that mean?" I don't know.
If you were her age you were fighting
For cover, not out arming yourself.

2.
When other towns died, ours buzzed.
Food we associated with home choked its air.
The one break from our eye-ball to eye-ball
Was for paper plates heaped and steaming:
Lashings of pepper, mouth water, sasparilla
To wash it down—"man can't think on hungry belly."
The best smoke came after we caned the meal,
A lull that picked-up full throttle.

We emerged to frosted cars and the uniform dark
Terraced houses entertained; our long goodbyes
Reverberated; during the hop-in, hop-out drive
Or springy steps home, it could have been any
They pulled beside and bundled into the van
You'd be carried from, into the station, dead.

INTERVIEW/FRED D'AGUIAR

The very choice of title says a lot, does'nt it? 'Frontline Chronicle' leaves the reader in no uncertain state about what you are going to say.

Absolutely. In 1981 when they had the great insurrections, the riots and so on across London, in Brixton, I was working at a hospital as a psychiatric nurse, and coming off duty I heard on the radio that Brixton was burning, and I used to go to a writing workshop there once a week, and I couldn't associate the uprising and the troubles in the streets with this place where I cycled to a workshop to learn about writing. And while saying that, at the same time, the debates that came out of the troubles with the police were actually debates that were going on in the workshop all the time—about language, about acceptability, about an establishment in poetry, about harassment and what subjects can get into poems and what can't, and who controls customs of the imagination and who polices it. All kinds of debates actually raging in the workshop and somehow we didn't connect these debates with the real world outside. So 'frontline' alludes to the fact that Brixton is called the frontline, but also to the fact blacks, as an ethnic/racial group and in terms of economics at the moment in Britain, are certainly on the frontline. You know, you go for a job and if you're black, you know, all the usual things: prejudice just based on skin colour, that's really shocking.

Having all these thoughts in your mind, how did you actually begin?

Usually I begin with a line or an image. The image, I think, was the idea of the row around a table, this debate. It's really about styles of writing, because at that time I was into very flowery poetry that really came from Wordsworth and some of my mates were writing very urban poems. So the debate was about what you must say. I was defending the imagination, had some kind of woolly notion of the imagination, and they were saying rubbish, if you go out into the streets and you get hit by a baton or you get called a certain name, that must enter your poems. And so I wanted to get that battle in the poem between nature and the city almost.

But the airship, the first sort of military reference, is a dated reference.

24

Terribly. Whilst they were talking about truncheons and racism, I had to say, well, my way of writing is actually to refer to a past that isn't even located here, Guyanese. Not only that, it's also a memory. My grandmother actually told us this memory: she actually stoned these big airships that we called blimps. She was out there doing this while everyone else was diving for cover, and I was very impressed with this young woman doing this thing. And that's the memory that came to me: the idea of resistance seemed to be in this image. So my way of entering this subject wasn't through these great debates, but to have this straightforward memory and try to represent that as some image of defence. I felt that for me a way into the contemporary issue had to be grounded on experience partially, and if my experience wasn't all that direct then I had to look somewhere else for it.

Carol Ann Duffy

MRS SKINNER, NORTH STREET

Milk bottles. Light through net. No post. Cat,
come here by the window, settle down. Morning
in the street awakes unwashed; a stale wind
breathing litter, last night's godlessness. This place
is hellbound in a handcart, Cat, you mark
my words. Strumpet. Slut. A different man
for every child and not a shred of shame.

My dentures grin at me, gargling water
on the mantelpiece. The days are gone
for smiling, wearing them to chatter down the road.
Good morning. Morning. Lovely day. Over the years
I've suffered loss, bereavement, loneliness.
A terrace of strangers. An old ghost
mouthing curses behind a cloudy, nylon veil.

Scrounger. Workshy. Cat, where is the world
I married; was carried into up a scrubbed stone step?
The young louts roam the neighbourhood.
Breaking of glass. Chants. Sour abuse of aerosols.
That social worker called me *xenophobic*. When she left,
I looked the word up. Fear, morbid dislike, of strangers.
Outside, the rain pours down relentlessly.

People scurry for shelter. How many hours
have I sat here, Cat, filled with bitterness
and knowing they'll none of them come?
Not till the day the smell is noticed.
Not till the day you're starving, Cat, and begin
to lick at my corpse. I twitch at this curtain
as the Asian man next door runs through the rain.

INTERVIEW/CAROL ANN DUFFY

Tell me how this poem began.

I was in the north of England, in Bolton, Lancashire, giving poetry readings in schools. A lot of the schools were in run-down parts of that town, and at lunchtime I would walk round these areas. In this particular street called North Street—the title of the poem—there was always a slightly crazy, bad-tempered looking old lady, peeping out through the net curtains, mouthing at people, banging on the door if children were playing games near her, on the doorstep. Quite an extraordinary woman. And that kind of drew me in to thinking about that particular street and that particular woman. I noticed that she had a cat in the window with her, and she would stroke the cat whilst glaring at the world outside. So obviously the cat was very important, and probably her only company. I tried very hard to describe the environment she was in—dirt, litter, graffiti, and hers the only clean step—and to invent a likely emotional state for her. She is a woman who, in a sense, is without neighbours. Although she is racist and anti-children, she is in fact talking about her neighbours. She is linked to them by dislike rather than liking.

One thing that must strike the reader or listener almost immediately, is the contrast between the everyday language of the woman talking to her cat, mixed with the more poetic language that she couldn't possibly use herself, things like "hellbound in a handcart".

I'd have to disagree with you there: this is something that's actually said in that part of England. If you have a quarrel with someone, it's very common to say, well, they can go to hell in a handcart. If someone had taken to drink, they would be hellbound in a handcart. So that is, I feel, the kind of language she would use. As is "strumpet". I mean that's not a word I would use, but it is a slightly archaic word for, I don't know, loose woman; we'd probably say "slag" or something equally vile now. The one thing she probably wouldn't say—when she's looking for her false teeth on the mantlepiece—she wouldn't say they were "gargling water". That's me as the poet imposing that. But I think you can do that as long as the poem is balanced.

What does "godlessness" signify?

Drinking, going with boys, anything that a very strict old lady of about 90 would find shocking. Going to pubs, discos, wearing short skirts and makeup. She's talking to the cat.

What about "Scrounger. Workshy" in the third stanza?

"Scrounger. Workshy" is referring to someone she sees on the street, perhaps a man who is coming out of a betting shop, when she thinks it's three o'clock in the afternoon, he should be at work. "Strumpet" is a woman she sees walking down the street with a couple of children. The woman might have a black child and a white child, and she doesn't approve of that.

"Sour abuse of aerosols"?

That's me slightly taking control of the poem, rather than the woman's voice. She's annoyed at messages, slogans sprayed by aerosols, annoyed at vandalism, breaking of glass, chanting of gang and football slogans.

In the final stanza—"How many hours/have I sat here, Cat, filled with bitterness/ and knowing they'll none of them come?"—who does she mean by "they"?

In my mind it was perhaps her family—it's a very common problem for old people is loneliness and not being visited. It's also being extended to the very people she's mouthing curses at. Although she feels free to disapprove of them, she's perhaps aware that her disapproval and unfriendliness would mean that they wouldn't knock on her door and say 'How are you for milk, Mrs Skinner?' She's driven them away. And "Not till the day the smell is noticed"—perhaps quite a shocking line—is again a common thing: people can be dead in their houses for weeks, and the neighbours never knew. It happens all the time.

U. A. Fanthorpe

photo by R. V. Bailey

NEIGHBOURS

The Collared couple lived at number one,
In the guttering. They were good neighbours,
Kept an orderly house, the missus was always home.
They might have been R.C. Her tender nape
Bent over her brood was slightly Madonna-ish,
And the three notes they chanted all day, all day,
Some kind of psalm?

Ivy made the gable a high-rise ghetto;
The Blackies at 1b were a racketty lot.
Kept odd hours, zoomed home like motorbikes revving,
Tried to mug the Collareds, at the least excuse
Would scream blue murder, threaten to call the cops.
It was because of them the cat left home.

Our next-door neighbours keep themselves to themselves.
We swap small talk and seedlings over the fence
Sometimes, but not too often. You have to keep
A certain distance.

Two terrorists at large in our neighbourhood
Must have holed up somewhere close. We haven't seen them.
Our neighbours have. *Her*, with her kill,
Standing as if at home on the compost heap,
One foot upraised to pluck. She didn't move,
Outstared them till they backed into the house.
They talk of her yellow eyes, her butcher's poise,
The pigeon bleeding in her taloned fist.

To be a sparrowhawk's neighbour is an honour,
And yet the harmless squabs and fledgling blacks
(Her prey) are neighbours too. We let them be,
And then she guts them for the fluffy brood
She nurtures with the awesome tenderness
We see on television.   We don't say this
To our human neighbours, not-quite-friends,
In case they think we're soft. You have to keep
A certain distance.

31

INTERVIEW/U. A. FANTHORPE

Can I begin by asking you about this area where you live?

Well, it's a very well-birded part of Gloucestershire. We have buzzards up the hill, and sparrowhawks around, as you gather.

You choose, in fact, to talk about feathered neighbours. What about real neighbours? Is it a neighbourly area?

Oh, very neighbourly. Except that, it's safer, somehow, to become friends with people who don't live too close. I think they think that. And, of course, I didn't want to do the obvious thing, the good samaritan, the idea of helpfulness throughout the world — not that I wouldn't like to write about it—but I thought lots of other people will write about that.

What came first?

I began with the birds I was most intimately involved with, the collared doves and the blackbirds, and then our neighbour did tell me about the sparrowhawk. I saw straight away that I would like to play around with the blackbirds, in the way people call them "Blackies" and so on. I think I was leading up to that with "the Collared couple".

Why are they called "collared"? Do you know?

Yes, they've got a little black mark that goes right round the back of their neck.

The reference to "R.C."?

Roman Catholics.

And then you continue this reference with "Her tender nape", that's her neck, "Bent over her brood was slightly Madonna-ish", again picking up the Roman Catholic reference, carried on into the chanting.

Yes, actually it's a rather maddening noise that they make, but I've sort of sanctified it for them.

Tell me about "Ivy made the gable as high-rise ghetto".

32

Well, the gable is the right-hand wall of our garden, and the ivy was very attractive to birds and therefore a lot of them were nesting there, so I thought of it as a ghetto with so many bird families packed in.

And "a racketty lot"?

The noisy blackbirds are based on my boss when I worked at a hospital. She lived in a council house next door to a house where the husband had died and all the sons had gone wild, and this is a more-or-less detailed account of how they behaved.

What do you mean by "To be a sparrowhawk's neighbour is an honour"?

Well, they were one of the birds, like most birds of prey, that were affected by the DDT used on farms, and I think it's splendid that such birds as peregrines, buzzards, and sparrowhawks have come back to Gloucestershire.

"We let them be,/And then she guts them for the fluffy brood" etc. Would you talk me through that? Quite a gruesome contrast there.

This is something I think we're awfully lucky about, the way that television shows us things in the nest and the burrow that previous generations just hadn't seen, or only gamekeepers, maybe. And there is, I think, something very special about the way in which all birds of prey bend over to feed their young. They don't regurgitate, they actually bring the stuff in their claws. But there's the same kind of tenderness which I think I mention with the collared dove. We don't mention all these irreconcilable feelings that we have about sparrowhawks and their prey to our human neighbours because it's too complicated a matter.

GLOSSARY
"racketty" (line 9): suggestive both of noise and criminal activity.
"mug" (line 11): attack to rob, usually applied to attacking old people.
"scream blue murder" (line 12): shout out loudly for help.
"squabs" (line 27): young pigeons.
"fledgling blacks" (line 27): baby blackbirds too young to fly.

Stuart Henson

NEIGHBOURS

These two were neighbours fifty years,
who leaned across the new wire fence
in 1943 and joked and frowned at whitefly
in the cabbages. They'd wipe their brows;
one spoke, one laughed, admired the rows—
first flowering of the Dig for Victory.

An age then of spare utility: the flat
square bungalows with geometric frames
that sprouted on the field-edge overnight,
that in a month were homes and lives,
not rich but busy, and not blighted yet
but pinched with a war austerity.

Clear afternoons they'd push back from their spades
and watch the sky grow black with Fortresses
turning and droning like a hive of bees
put up to swarm and settle on Berlin.
Then shadows flitted on the mind of nights
to come, in wet tin shelters, cowering.

And yet, they say, these two old men
who sit and gaze out from their bench
half drowsy with the sun and age,
those were the days, the good old days,
when families next door sat round a lamp,
sang worn-out songs to drown the raids.

Reels, reels of memory, of VE Day: a whole street
drunk in each others' arms on nothing more
than pure relief. All this and then
decades of peace: the century unwinding
on a slow downhill from ration-book to pension-book,
and illnesses, and the gardens left to weeds.

These two were neighbours fifty years:
their houses were a temporary affair
that lingered after skies had cleared
and the world spun on. Yet still at night
their lighted window-squares share one black roof,
fixed by the small sharp nail-heads of stars.

INTERVIEW/STUART HENSON

The neighbours that you mention at the beginning of the poem—to what extent were they your neighbours?

The old men of the poem are imaginary figures, though they could be many individuals. Two old men I imagine sitting on a bench in the sunshine. I did use images which were from conversations with my own neighbours—the image of the aeroplanes, the American bombers, the Fortresses, which in the poem rise up from the airfield near my home in a village called Kimbolton in Huntingdonshire. That image of the planes rising like a swarm of bees was one actually spoken to me by one of my neighbours who lived during the Second World War in the street where I live.

Do you have the feeling that the war still exerts a strong influence on you, or perhaps on this generation you're talking about?

I think it does. I was born in 1954, and in a way I suppose the poem tries to tell a little of the social history of England. I tried, in the image of "a slow downhill from ration-book to pension-book", to imagine the lives which in a way were blighted by the war, that were not begun fully, and then which follow in this second half of the twentieth century, in a way towards the materialism which we have substituted perhaps for the intimacy and the community and the neighbourliness which I chose to find a focus in during wartime, during the sheltering from the air raids in the Anderson shelters.

And yet it's slightly regrettable that people should be brought together because of some external threat.

Indeed, yes. In the poem I've tried to point that up by looking at the sky twice. Looking at the sky in the first instance filled with the planes of the American 8th Air Force, which were stationed here in Britain ostensibly to help in the defence of Britain, but which were in fact inflicting heavy

36

bombing on the cities of Europe, and then to see that reciprocity in the moment of the shadow flitting across the lives of the ordinary people who are digging their gardens, digging in order to produce more food to feed the nation, the campaign to "Dig for Victory" I mention in the first stanza. I imagine seeing those planes the two neighbours would be immediately reminded of their own fear when the planes of the German Air Force made their reciprocal raids on Britain. And then at the close of the poem I tried to look up to those skies which have cleared, and to the larger roof, the great black roof of the night sky, which at one time carried with it the terror of the bombing, and now, I hope, covers both the neighbours in the immediate vicinity, whose windows are lit up, and those people in those European cities who perhaps were equally innocent victims of the history of that time.

There's a certain gentleness, a softness and a tenderness about the description of these characters, and yet right at the end, just when you think you can relax, suddenly you've got this hard image—"the small sharp nail-heads of stars".

I was trying to evoke a sense of construction, of human endeavour, the nailing together, the piecing together of a roof, in this case a roof which is fixed with something solid. The stars to me are always an image of security. I don't know why that should be, but to look up at the stars seems to me very often to give a sense of peace, which I hope the gentleness of the poem evokes. To use that image of nail-heads, the light perhaps glinting on a nail or pin which has been used to secure something, seemed to me appropriate to the kind of emotion I was trying to convey.

GLOSSARY
"spare utility" (line 7): without luxury. "Utility furniture" was cheap, very basic furniture produced in wartime.

Keith Howden

NEIGHBOURS

They claimed the moor for neighbour, etched their farms
—*Rake Head, Windy Harbour*—in acid parishes
where vision led. Names gaunt with truth dissenting
the seasons' rituals, crude as wind ranting
its barren testaments, Faith's harbingers, they preached
labour's utilitarian religion.

Trespassed their neighbour's cloisters, sacked his shrines
—*Nut Shaw, Barley Top*—where they commanded
walls built to stem or swerve his sour recoil.
Syllables relevant as famine; each name
the thing it was, security against
the moor's revenges. They staked his land their own.

These were their lime evangelism's chapels
—*Stone Fold, Wet Head*—faith's proper prisons;
sites christened by the land's austerity.
With pulpit vowels, hallelujah consonants
denied the moor's religion, raised their psalms
apostate in their neighbour's mysteries.

Bibles of picks and ploughs they consecrated
—*Old Barn, New Barn*—names nodding at hunger.
From laagered missions, won among the infidel
intake, some scattered gestures of conversion.
Nothing recanted. No miracle redeemed
indigenous atheism in the grass.

The bald moor holds them now. The leper-stations
—*Cronkie, White Riding*—where vision foundered,
stand sepulchres to that dead neighbourhood
gospelled in names. Nobody stayed. No labour
prospered to breach the moor's truth. Nothing appeased
a god dissolved in different sacraments.

INTERVIEW/KEITH HOWDEN

Could you encapsulate in one sentence, not the meaning of the poem—that's too complex—but some help to the listener who hears the poem only once?

Yes. I would say that, while on its surface it appears to be a visual poem about a landscape, it's really about some of the deeper preoccupations that landscape stirs in me.

Can you tell me what inspired you, how the poem began?

Yes, it's beginnings are the most obvious ones for a poet. It's where I lived, it's where I first experienced the world. Some of my relatives lived in one of these farms, and it's the landscape I'm most fond of.

How did the two ideas come together, the moors and the neighbours?

I was interested in the fact that these communities formed what appeared to be neighbours, that they appeared to be in some kind of neighbourhood with the moor, but in fact they were part of an opposition rather than a neighbourhood, and it's that sense of neighbourhood and non-neighbourhood which I wanted to exploit.

Who are "they" at the beginning?

"They" are the farmers, the people who have settled in these fairly windy and wild outposts in their attempts to bring a pretty recalcitrant nature under control.

Could you describe the landscape for somebody who doesn't know the Lancashire moors?

It's that landscape of broken walls, bald hills, flat millstone bricktops above the moors, lonely farms above the industrial valleys. It's a landscape, for me at least, redolent with both history and emotion.

The farms will be farms producing what?

Producing nothing now: indeed that sense of a neighbourhood that would produce nothing is part of the atmosphere.

The names of the farms are real names, taken from your own knowledge?

Taken from my own knowledge, but I certainly had to go to the Ordnance Survey map of the 1880s, I think, primarily because they were names I knew from my mother and my grandfather telling me the names. I knew the farms themselves, but I had to use the map to find what the names had been. The names of the farms form a kind of refrain. I was interested in the names. They have a kind of existential quality in that there's nothing here that suggests the human, only Old Barn and New Barn later on. The names are merely descriptive: here I am and what I am: Blake Head, Windy Harbour, Barley Top.

A bitter simile, isn't it, "relevant as famine"?

Again, if I may go on about it, you see, Barley Top, which appears to suggest richness, is actually nothing to do with barley, but is 'bare lea' where nothing grows. And in that sense, and in their modern appearance, the sense that nothing did grow, nothing did hold, was part of the bitter suggestion.

You use a very hard-sounding language, Anglo-Saxon expressions and Biblical terms.

Almost the whole language of the poem takes words that I would almost certainly associate with the kind of religion I knew on those moors, but without accepting it. The poem is about a conflict of religious attitudes: as the farms impose themselves on the moors, so certain kinds of attitude have always tried to impose themselves on the spiritual climate.

GLOSSARY
"These were their lime evangelism's chapels" (line 13): Lime was used to sweeten the acid moor. In a sense, as they spread the lime, they spread their gospel.
"apostate" (line 18): heretic.
"laagered" (line 21): fenced-in defensively.

John Latham

A FAMOUS DANCER

For weeks we couldn't tell
if the curtains really twitched
each time we passed or shouted:
Miss Lloyd, recluse for thirty years,
who used to be a famous dancer,
but was sadly disappointed
—Mrs Greenleaves told us—by a man:
though not, we thought, her brother,
wobbling on his bike to Mr Daly's shop,
and back, more slowly, basket laden.

One day, her nose appeared, suspicious,
some weeks afterwards, her chin,
and by summer, the top half of her,
hand clutching the curtains,
breath-ghosts on the window,
glasses blaring if the sun was low.
At first, when we waved to her
she shrank into the velvet,
but by August she just stiffened,
as if a thought had struck her.

The street responded. Mrs Abel waved,
Miss Maddock twirled her stick,
Mr Capper moved his hand like Jesus:
'She's coming back', my mother said.
On New Year's Eve I whistled,
her curtains soared away. Swaying,
naked, she was smiling at the sky.
I fled, found Mr Lloyd. He nodded,
stroked his bell. 'Don't worry, lad.
She used to be a famous dancer'.

INTERVIEW/JOHN LATHAM

Could you tell me what part of the country this is, where the poem is set?

I grew up, and this poem is essentially set, in what was then rather a small, agricultural village in Cheshire called Frodsham, which is not far from Chester. A population then probably of 3,000 or so.

This incident as described in the poem would have created quite an impact at the time?

Yes, I think it would, because it was a sufficiently small and intimate community that everyone knew everyone else, even the recluses like Miss Lloyd. I've used real names—I find it impossible not to, somehow, in writing poetry. But I have distorted the story somewhat. Miss Lloyd herself is, I think, some kind of composite of two or three people whom I felt I knew when I was a child.

What age were you, roughly, when this happened?

I can imagine that this relates to my being 8 or 9 years old.

And who was she, this Miss Lloyd, was she in fact a famous dancer?

No, that's fictitious. There was a lady who lived along the road that I lived in, who spent her day behind the curtains, and the evolution of her contact with the real world I think was approximately described here, in that she did eventually gain confidence and blossom. Another lady in town, an old lady, is the one who actually exposed herself. She exposed herself to a group of kids when she was becoming senile. So I combined these two women in the one story.

What was the effect on you as kids?

We were cruel. I think children are cruel. We just pointed and laughed, and she was shocked and embarrassed. It was only later, though, that I realised just how callous we'd been.

In the second stanza there's a reference to her standing by the window, and you talk about "breath-ghosts" on the window. Could you explain?

The idea there is someone standing very close to a window, to the inside of the window, breathing on to it, so presumably the glass would have to be colder. So it's probably cold outside, and condensation from the breath makes these patches which are about face size, which erode pretty quickly from the outside in. So they are ephemeral and ghostly in the sense that you can see through them somewhat.

Her glasses were "blaring". That's a strong word.

Yes, it may be too strong a word. Physically, what I think I'm referring to is if the sun's fairly low, then at particular angles you get very strong reflection. It would seem then as almost the equivalent of a trumpet coming from this room, and that might fit in the sense that, although she is being furtive and wishes to be concealed, my knowing that she was there made her become a very strong presence in fact, and sometimes almost an overwhelming one. And so the "blaring" perhaps conveys the impossibility of going past that house sometimes without feeling her staring.

What do you mean by "'She's coming back', my mother said"?

I think I meant it in the sense that perhaps after all these years Miss Lloyd was gaining the confidence to perhaps even enter again into the society which hadn't dropped her and tried to continue making contact with her, but wasn't able to do so except through this window at this stage. So yes, a comeback, a social comeback.

GLOSSARY
"twitched" (line 2): implies a sudden, jerky movement with the further implication of a sense of excitement and lack of control in the person moving the curtain.
"recluse" (line 4): someone who leads a solitary life, shut away from normal life.

photo by Robert Burns

Norman MacCaig

NEIGHBOUR

His car sits outside the house.
It never goes anywhere, is it
a pet?

When he goes for this morning paper
he makes a perfect rightangle
at the corner.

What does he do at home? Sit at attention?
Or does he stay in the lobby
like a hatstand?

Does his wife know she married
a diagram? That she goes to bed
with a faded blueprint?

When I meet him
he greets me with a smile
he must have bought somewhere.

His eyes are two teaspoons
that have been emptied
for the last time.

INTERVIEW/NORMAN MACCAIG

I'd like to ask you about the person in this poem.

In the first place, he isn't my nearest neighbour. I wouldn't like my nearest neighbour to hear this poem and suppose it's about him. The one I was thinking of lives up the street. He's like a robot, a mechanical man. I can imagine him having a key in his back that his wife screws up every morning to keep him going through the day. Very remote person.

When you wrote the poem, did you start off with the first line? Can you remember now how it took shape?

I always start off with the first line. I always start at the beginning and end at the end. Often it doesn't take any longer to write the poem than it would be for me to copy it out. Often no changes at all. People say, "How long does it take you to write a poem, Norman?", and I say, "two cigarettes". All that sounds marvellous, doesn't it? There's a snag, of course—there's always a snag. I write a lot that I throw in the wastepaper basket.

Could you say something about the people who live in your part of Edinburgh?

Well, this part of Edinburgh is solidly bourgeois, middle-class, money enough to be comfortable, but certainly not rich. Nice people. No muggings go on in Leamington Terrace.

The neighbour in the poem, what is his main failing?

Well, I think it's very clearly a sad inability to communicate with other people. He's a very lonely man. I'm sorry for him. I make a joke of him in the poem, but in fact I'm very sorry for him. He's locked up in himself, he can't communicate with people. Which is very sad, isn't it? Because communicating with people is the most important thing in one's life. People are far more important than poetry.

Could you tell me about some of the references in this poem, for someone who perhaps doesn't understand them? "Faded blueprint"?

A blueprint is a drawing scheme for some project like making a bolt or building a building. The architects make what is called a blueprint, a plan.

And in this case "a faded *blueprint"?*

Well, he once had the chance of becoming a building, that's to say of becoming a real man, a real human being who could talk to other ones. But the building was never erected from the blueprint.

The teaspoons?

Well, his eyes are dead cold, and he always walks looking straight ahead. You think he's seeing nothing, he's lost—that's a failing too. He seems to have lost interest even in the outside world. So that the two eyes that we all have, if we're lucky, give us great social knowledge, of course. But he's ceased to use them, so they're like two teaspoons that have been empty for ages.

When I read the poem, my feeling about it was that it was very funny.

Well, it is, of course, a caricature, and it's meant to be. It's meant to be a slightly joky poem, slightly funny poem. It wouldn't be unfair to say that it was a caricature of a man.

Julian May

CUTTING THE BORDER WIRES

'Good fences make good neighbours' — Robert Frost

By the time I reached Inner Mongolia
          I was not well;
I curled up in the doorway of the yurt
          and watched the grasslands roll
like a sea from the horizon to my feet,
          Then I was home

until a fighter razor-slashed the sky
          and terrified the small community of crows.
But the camel merely raised his quivering nose
          and spat his cruds of half-chewed grass.
Bagen explained the border was close by,
          how one day he would cut that wire,
drive his flock to Ulan Bator and greet his people there
          (he called them *neighbours I have never seen*).

Fleeing Tel Aviv, they dragged me from the queue and fired
          questions till they thought I'd had enough
and let me drop. In Peking they locked me up,
          exposed my films.
At midnight somewhere beneath Berlin the dog snapped and the
          soldier snarled
          because my foot strayed across the line.
Every country's border guards bark the same foreign language;
          I'm fluent now;
coming in at Harwich I understood their finger-pointing.
          It said *You've cut too many wires*.

So home in this Tottenham street I'm digging in,
          I'm mending fences
between strange neighbours who have travelled far too far
          and need to keep their boundaries.
But the walls between our lives are thin
          as canvas;

Beata croons soft Polish,
                    Manuel knows only Spanish when he loves.
The Greeks advise me how to tend the vine but never speak
                    to the hospitable Turks
though the smoking spitting savour of their barbecues
                    melts all our walls.
In midwinter Rufus shivered at the door,
                    Just come roun say g'bye. I had it
wi dis weather, man. I gwan home. To Jamaica!
                    Like mango, man? I send you mango.
Have tree in mi backyard make mango
                    taste of sunshine.
Gwan lean against mi tree, soak up dat sun
                    like ol tortoise, till I die.

Now Rufus has gone the summer's come to my fenced-in backyard;
                    I'm digging in a mango stone for him.
Across the street three supple Filipino children
                    slash the quiet with their cricket.
A Sikh bowler lets fly to a skinhead batsman
                    and Mohammed takes the perfect catch.
The Turks are cooking in their garden,
                    somewhere reggae drums are talking
and the night is hot. I fling up the bedroom window,
                    soak it in.

INTERVIEW/JULIAN MAY

This is an amazingly global, sort of comprehensive poem—much more so than any of the other poems, which have tended to concentrate either on their own world or on a larger world. Can you tell me first about your own neighbours?

When I wrote the poem I was living in Tottenham, in north London, and the neighbours are actually those I describe in the poem. It was a very cosmopolitan area.

It doesn't sound as if it was a neighbourly area, was it?

I think it was actually fairly neighbourly. What there was there was a respect for people's privacy. I think that the epigraph from Robert Frost's poem "Mending Walls"—"good fences make good neighbours"—is true: in order to have good relationships you need to have some kind of division, I think. Now that's rather sad, and one sometimes has to break through—one has to cut the wires—and that's what the poem's dealing with, really. And I think in the last stanza of the poem I'm doing that. I actually saw a Sikh, a white skinhead and a Muslim boy all playing together. And I found that very encouraging. Also I feel that there might be some wishful thinking. One has to remember that in 1985 in Tottenham there was a terrible riot. Race was an important factor in that riot and neighbours were not living well with one another; a policeman was hacked to death. But in the street where I lived, which was only about a mile from where the riot took place, things weren't so bad, and we were getting on all right with our neighbours.

What about the other neighbours—the world family? Are they part of your direct experience?

Yes. I mean the poem is a traveller's tale; it's about coming home. And everything that happened in this poem is true. The jet plane made me think about divisions between countries, about borders and people having to defend borders. I always have difficulty crossing borders. When I go into another country and I have to show my passport, I always feel slightly nervous, slightly uneasy, and people pick up on that: I'm always the one who gets his bag searched. And I find it very worrying, really. So one feels slightly the outsider. And after you've done this, after you've travelled to Inner Mongolia, and you've been in Peking, Israel, Berlin—another divided city—the idea was I was coming home to Tottenham and that I was going to stop, and I was going to mend my fences between my neighbours and myself.

GLOSSARY
"yurt" (line 3): a round, felt tent with a conical roof and a hole in the top to let out smoke. Mongolians live and cook in these tents which can be packed up and carried away on a horse or camel.
"At midnight somewhere beneath Berlin" (line 19): you can go from East Berlin to West Berlin on the underground.

photo by Christopher Barker

Elma Mitchell

54

NEIGHBOURS

The walls are thin.
Everything I have, you have,
And *vice versa*.

We pick the same, or similar
Programmes out of the air

And our well-worn
Underpants, pegged to the whirling lines,
Semaphore understandably to each other.

We nod, smile,
Swap newspapers, and recommend, or damn,
Our choice of library books.

Alike, discreetly different,
Our zipped-up jackets and substantial shoes
Shut us impenetrably, imperturbably, in.

Our human line
Of communication's thin
But tough
Enough
As the days and the years draw on
To keep us from the slowly encroaching cold.

We know each other, of middle age, of old,
And smile and nod, and hold
To what we know
(Or wouldn't want to know).

The walls are thin—
Sensitive and impermeable as skin.

INTERVIEW/ELMA MITCHELL

How much of this is you? Is it where you live?

No, it's not where I live now. If anything, it's urban or suburban; it's true of small towns also. It is really about the British person's probable (but how do I know?) attitude to his neighbour. He wants to know just so much about him, but not too much.

What came first in this particular poem?

The phrase "the walls are thin". When you look at the structure of the poem, such as it is, you can see that it's enclosed between these walls. Obviously, the idea of being enclosed—in their clothes, in their walls, and so on—is a very strong one in the poem. It wasn't, of course, a personal poem, but it took that form.

Let's just have a look at some of the words and expressions you have chosen here. What is the "everything" in "The walls are thin./Everything I have, you have,/ And vice versa"?

To start with, the body and bones, of course; and the set-up: we're both human beings and, basically speaking, it's two people of the same—not exactly standard of living, but, roughly, way of living—they both wear fairly respectable clothes and so forth. They are like those little paper men that you unfold—you know, they join hands and one will fold on top of the other. You look round a railway carriage and you see the same thing, but you know perfectly well that they *are* different from each other and also that they would all rush to help if there were an accident—but they are darned if they are going to say a word to each other so long as there isn't!

And these two or three or however many people listen to the programmes? You mean, literally, radio programmes?

Yes—the same radio programmes; they probably listen to the news and other similar programmes. They have similar tastes and habits.

Up to now, and including the fourth stanza, which is the one about nodding and smiling and swapping newspapers, everything seems fine—and then suddenly there's a change of mood when you say "Alike" (rather deceptive this) and then "discreetly different,/Our zipped-up jackets and substantial shoes/Shut us impenetrably, imperturbably in". Things change there.

56

Yes, that is a sort of turning-point in the poem. By the "zipped-up jackets and substantial shoes" they are enclosed, away from each other, and that is really a sort of metaphor for the state of mind: thus far, and no further.

But "substantial" has all sorts of connotations, doesn't it? Practical, country shoes.

And the water won't get into your shoes, so that you are capable of keeping the world at bay, the messier parts of it, anyway. You can read a lot into that, if you like!

Tell me about "Our human line/Of communication's thin". Again, "line" has lots of meanings.

Yes: there's the simple idea of a sort of life-line that saves you, and the line of your life. As we get older, we're more aware of our separation from other people, *and* of our likeness to them, and then we say "We know each other". It's not a very profound knowing, but it's familiar.

I must say I like this use of "of old", which has two meanings. Could you, finally, expand on the use of the word "impermeable"?

Well, it means "cannot be penetrated" really. At least, it can be penetrated, by a knife or by something brutal, but not by liquid and not by touch—and therefore each feels safe within the skin. But the skin remains "sensitive"—it conveys to us the temperature outside, what is happening, and whether it has been touched or not touched. So that seems to be how the relationship stands.

Graham Mort

NEIGHBOURS

Fifteen floors high, these flats pile
Family above family and hold us there
Between the hunger-cries of gulls;
Only glass shields us from their wings,
Refracts their ravenous eyes.

An acid wind ulcerates our views,
Throwing pedestrians to the roads,
Litter across allotments where stray
Dogs shit and snarl and battle
Towards the butcher's dustbins.
Cars beach themselves at shops:
Their cargoes spill over back seats
Where abandoned children reach out
From their harnesses and howl.

Each night streetlamps, like
Lymphocytes, engulf the stars;
Televisions blare, sleepers turn,
The neurotic flares of music
Burning their blood to ash.

Each morning we leave our rooms,
Afraid to meet silences
That prowl the empty,
Falling flight of stairs.

We pack the elevator's black walls:
Its hoarding of glass gives us back
Our faces like something hunted.
Only our shoulders touch,
Not our eyes which search the floor
For swallowed cries, evidence
Of lives that hurtle the long shaft.

INTERVIEW/GRAHAM MORT

This is a far cry from where you're living now isn't it?

Yes, the area I live in now is a village on the footslopes of the Three Peaks, just under Inglebury Hill. It's just a linear village that follows a stream up, until the valley narrows to the point where there can be no more houses.

Tell me about the neighbourhood described in the poem.

The background to the poem was when I first became a full-time writer and creative writing teacher. I got a residency in a group of schools and colleges in Scunthorpe, and what happened was I left my village and lived there during the week. I came home at weekends. In Scunthorpe I lived for the first time in a high-rise block of flats. I was amazed by the feeling of having people living underneath me, on all sides of me, and also above me. That was a very strange and striking business.

You used neutral terms there, but your poem's not neutral.

No, I hated it! What struck me was the irony, between the idea of neighbours as I would know it in a Dales village, where we do actually know a great deal about each other and people are very interested in each other's lives, and suddenly being stuck in this high-rise block, where the whole idea of neighbourliness was non-existent. I lived there for five weeks before I saw the man who lived next door to me. So there was absolutely no contact between people. It seemed to me that the only point at which we came together was in the lift, this black box that travelled up and down this shaft in the middle of the flats. I thought that irony was something I wanted to explore.

You quite carefully avoid apportioning blame to anybody for the state of the lives of these people, the residents.

I think there's a sort of helplessness. I felt that people weren't in control of their own lives. Scunthorpe is very much a town that was built by town planners with some architectural philosophy that people could live like this. I think people in that situation suffer from this helplessness and alienation, from each other and from their surroundings as well.

So you feel they were and are victims?

Yes, I think so.

Can we look now at some of the references you make? Could you explain "An acid wind ulcerates our views"?

I wanted to get over the idea of the elements seeming to be burning from within, like a duodenal ulcer. And the earth there was very much scabbed and pockmarked. And that idea of the wind as a kind of chemical process eating away at the surroundings, that idea of erosion was very strong.

Tell me about "Each night streetlamps, like/Lymphocytes, engulf the stars".

In the body's immune system the lymphocytes are the white cells which engulf bacteria. Here I've really turned the image on its head—the streetlamps are literally swallowing the stars that should be there, that should be there over us. It's again that shutting out of the natural world by this structure that has been built artificially.

This metaphor is continued in the next few lines, with televisions as well: "neurotic flares of music/Burning their blood to ash".

The image I'm striving at there was this amazing business of lying awake in bed—I found it almost impossible to sleep with people all around —and all the time there was music coming from above and below and all sides. When you woke it was with that feeling of being consumed, of being used up by sleep, rather than being rested. There was this horrible kind of ashen grey feeling to the mornings when you got up. In the final verse suddenly we're looking at ourselves in that landscape very clearly. That's the inescapable process of the poem, that ultimately we need to look at ourselves in that situation. I think that's the first step towards doing something about it.

GLOSSARY
"allotments" (line 8): groups of rented vegetable gardens on a plot of land away from houses. They look like a patchwork of tiny fields and have huts and greenhouses on them.

M. R. Peacocke

NAMELESS

I do not know her name.
Clearing the trough, I found
her shadow, and wore it home.
Our steps moved easily
over the broken ground,
flagstones, pineapple weed.
We paused to watch a lamb
and the first brimstone butterfly
gladdening in the sun.
    She is one and many,
my undiscerned companion;
evidence of her life
bits and pieces thrown away
or lost, like this garden fork
roughly forged, its handle gone,
under a litter of sycamore leaf
and nettle lightly buried.
    My hands like hers have thickened
hoping to mould time
into a good loaf;
like her I bend my back
to root out thistle and dock
and trap the rat that capers under the roof.
Jetsam on this land,
labouring to eke out the hay
through meagre February,
perhaps at best we learn
to stand and note the streak of lime
that shows where already starlings are raising a brood
in the wall badged with lichen.

INTERVIEW/M. R. PEACOCKE

Can you tell me a bit about the area in which you live—you live on a farm?

It's an old stone farm, very high up in the north-west of England, on the Pennines. It's sheep country, nobody farms there commercially.

Do you actually have neighbours?

There is one household about a quarter of a mile away. But what I was interested in here was in writing about neighbours not in space but in time: the people who have been living on my patch before, whom I don't know. And I don't know anything about them, except by the things they've left behind, like pieces of horse harness and rusted tools. The house had been cleared out, but those things were around. They made me think a lot about the people who had used them.

Do you feel the presence very strongly of these nameless neighbours?

Sometimes. I think it depends on the weather, because of the kind of place it is. One's life is very much directed by the weather. One's always looking to see what the day's going to be like, what's coming tomorrow, and I feel as though there have always been people doing that, and I'm among them.

I have a feeling that the seasons change throughout the poem.

I feel it's a spring poem. I wrote it in the spring, and I think that the things I describe like the pineapple weed and the brimstone butterfly are creatures of spring.

In what I think is the second stanza, what do you mean by "She is one and many"?

I haven't any one woman in mind. There may be different women belonging to different generations, but I think their lives must have been shaped in very much the same way; they belong to the same culture.

Could you explain the word "jetsam", in the last stanza, and why you use this word to refer to yourself?

Jetsam is floating stuff on the sea, which is thrown up by the tide onto the beach. It might be branches, it might be an old orange box, it might be some sort of treasure. You never know what you're going to find. I found my farm and went to live there by a whole chain of what seemed to be chances. I felt that probably other women who had lived there had come there similarly, by chance, by accident.

Do you still feel that you are jetsam?

I feel very much that I belong there, but also that I am temporary. What I do, however much energy and time I put into it, makes a very little scratch on the surface of the ground. This ground is marginal and is not tameable in the way that lower and more fertile ground can be.

Finally, you seem to say that what's left for us to take consolation from is the fact that we can "learn/to stand and note". What do you mean by this?

Well, the exciting thing I find in living this kind of life in such a place, is that living creatures are extraordinarily opportunist, and they make the most of everything. You think winter is never going to come to an end, and yet there is something in advance of spring, beginning to produce children, produce young. This is something which I find very exhilarating, that gives point to life. The word, I think, in that part that is important to me is the word "stand", because I think that it's important to do that, to take time to see what's happening, to know what's happening. It ties up with 'making a stand', showing courage, and withstanding the opposition of adverse forces. It ties up in my mind also with understanding. That standing is again something that takes time, and uses time.

GLOSSARY
"trough" (line 2): a water trough for animals.
"pineapple weed" (line 6): a very common weed which grows in gateways.
"brimstone butterfly" (line 8); a pale yellow butterfly that hatches out in early spring and seems to promise warm weather.
"eke out" (line 25): to make something last long enough for your purposes—the phrase always suggests that there isn't going to be enough. In this case not enough hay.

William Scammell

66

NEW NEIGHBOUR

Who say I must not
enter his house, but knock and wait.
He is for saving the whale. Other
causes clamour at his windows.
He favours pot, and impulse, and the bicycle;
rolls cigarettes called snout.
Bass guitars palpate the party wall.
He thinks we face extinction.
Dobbs wears beads, one silver earring
and a wrestler's chest, with which
he seals the doorway of my old friend's house.

INTERVIEW/WILLIAM SCAMMELL

Can I first of all ask you about the area in which you live?

I live in the Lake District, which is quite well-known as a tourist area. But I live in West Cumbria, which is a bit less touristy and a bit less visited. So I'm midway between the beauty spots and West Cumbria, which was once heavily industrialised and is now rather run-down.

In this poem you refer to a specific neighbour. Does he exist?

Yes, indeed! This poem is fairly unusual in that it's more or less a very straight and very direct transcription of an actual next-door neighbour, someone who moved in.

How do you think he would react on hearing this poem?

Not too pleased, I suspect. On the other hand, I thought his behaviour was such that in a way he deserved this poem to be written about him. I may say that this was written a little while ago now, and since then he has calmed down somewhat, and we are rather more friendly than we were to begin with. I think what made the whole experience a bit more abrupt for me was that previously a very close friend of mine had lived in the house.

The objection was primarily that he took the place of a friend, not that you felt he belonged to a different group? It wasn't that you were getting old and he was the new youth coming through?

Well, there may be an element of that. I suppose I was trying to place him in a certain category, a certain grouping.

There's a build-up in the description of the neighbour, bit by bit pieces come together. First of all, he's for saving the whale—what whale?

As you may know, whales have been hunted almost to extinction by various nations, and Greenpeace and other ecological groups have been saying for years and years now that we must stop killing whales at the rate we have been doing or there won't be any whales left. So all right-thinking people support this, and the even more right-thinking people put up posters and things in their windows, actually proclaiming SAVE THE WHALE, we must do something to save the whale.

68

But there is the implication there in the next line, "Other/causes clamour in his windows", that you suspect his motives, that he may be too genuine.

Yes, or there's a slightly satirical dig, perhaps, at those people who plaster their windows with all sorts of posters and all sorts of causes. The people who support many, many causes—it becomes a way of life, and I suppose I'm suspicious of people for whom causes become a way of life. There's a famous character in Dickens's novel *Bleak House*, a lady who has a husband and a large family, many children, all of whom she totally neglects because she spends all her time collecting money to send missionaries to Africa, and so on. Dickens has some fun with her on those grounds. I suppose in a small way I'm making a similar point. It's not that I'm impugning his motives or the causes—I think they're perfectly good causes—but I suppose there's a question of degree: how many causes you can support at any one time.

"He thinks we face extinction." What from?

This refers back partly to the line "Other/causes clamour at his windows". We live in Cumbria, and far and away the largest industry in Cumbria is British Nuclear Fuels, which reprocesses spent nuclear material from atomic stations and all sorts of places. There's been a lot of controversy about how safe British Nuclear Fuels is, and how much emission of waste matter and other radioactive material gets into the sea, into the air, into the grass, into the local milk, etc. So it's partly that, partly too, I suppose, that CND people think we face extinction in that there could be a nuclear accident.

In the final description you become much more precise about him—"Dobbs wears beads, one silver earring/and a wrestler's chest". It must be puzzling to listeners in some parts of the world—the earring, the beads. What sort of people wear these things?

I suppose I'm suggesting partly what type of person he is, and partly too perhaps, beneath all this I'm having a little dig at myself. I'm settling into middle age, arteries hardening etc. He represents youth. What he wears suggests someone who's deliberately flouting the bourgeois conventions.

GLOSSARY
"party wall" (line 7): the dividing wall between two houses in a terrace. Here there is also the suggestion of a party—drinking, dancing—going on next door.

Vernon Scannell

NEIGHBOURS

She:
'Leave, my love, before the morning
Drains the darkness from the pane.
Others who ignored this warning
Did not live to love again.

'Stars, those frozen birdsong fragments,
Soon will melt and disappear;
Footsteps on the frosty pavements
Tap out signals you should fear.'

He:
'How, my dearest, can I hasten
From your clinging limbs and lips
Now warm folds of blind sensation
Cause a rational eclipse?

'What if curtain-peeping neighbours
Recognise the man they see?
Let them wave their stage-prop sabres,
They can't injure you and me.'

She:
'Ah, my love, I fear night's ending
Not because your dawn-lit face
Would feed the need of those intending
Our exposure and disgrace.

'What I dread is our own gazing,
In the light that tells no lies,
At each other, neighbours, facing
Features we don't recognise.'

INTERVIEW/VERNON SCANNELL

Could you begin by describing the neighbourhood you live in at the moment?

Well, the neighbourhood I live in is a small market town in West Yorkshire, and has got little to do with this poem. I haven't any particular geographical place for this poem. If I had one at all, I think I was thinking of quite a big city, possible London.

But the neighbours you talk about here seem to be neighbours you could meet anywhere.

In the first part 'she' is certainly worried about the neighbours seeing her lover leaving, because they will form opinions—censorious opinions, probably—of their behaviour as lovers. It may possibly be an illicit relationship. It ends, of course, with the two of them neighbours in bed, in that sense.

Do you think this is a particular aspect of the English or British way of life?
I think this sort of curtain-peeping thing certainly happens in the suburbs and smaller towns of England. Yes, I think one is aware of a kind of prurient and inquisitive and quite probably rather judgemental or censorious interest in people's behaviour and neighbours' behaviour.

I'm very interested in the form you've chosen for the poem, which is, in a way, a sort of ballad. Not exactly a ballad—and I don't mean to say sing-song—but it's heavily rhythmic. I notice the end of each line—certainly the first and third in each stanza—is a falling rhyme. It's also an exchange; it's like so many of the old ballads where it's spoken by two different people. So it's in fact a little play, a conversational poem or dramatic poem, in that way.

Yes, I think that's right. It *is* dramatic and it's meant to be. It is a little dialogue, and as for the rhythm, it's written in fairly strictly trochaic metre. I was rather consciously getting away from the more common metre in English verse, the iambic movement. Also, I rather had the idea that it could possibly be set to music. I'd have quite liked to hear it sung. I imagine trochaic metre might lend itself easily to a musical setting.

This poem is very like a song in itself. It is in fact a tape recording, isn't it, of two lovers either talking or singing to each other of their fears and their doubts?

Yes, I know what you mean, the reader in a sense is overhearing this conversation, isn't there at all, but has got his ear to the bedroom wall, is eavesdropping in a sense.

Leaving aside the question of life, the question of poetry—it is often a fact that a female speaker in a poem will tend to be wiser and certainly more intuitive about the reality of the situation the poem sets up than the male protagonist. This poem seems to be in that tradition, which is rather like Hardy and a bit like Housman. It is a rather doom-filled poem, isn't it? I think that's something to do with the rhythm. I think if you use that trochaic rhythm, which is falling, falling, falling all the time, it does suggest that no good is going to come of this.

I think so, and I think that's what I was after.

Did you know how you were going to finish it when you started it, or did the poem grow as it went along?

I think like most poems, yes, if they're any good it's very rare to begin them up-ended. I think it was Robert Frost, the great American poet, who said that if there was no surprise for the writer there would be none for the reader. In other words, the writer, the poet, should surprise himself, should find the end of the poem has not been foreseen. And yet, when he arrives at it, there should be a certain inevitability about it. Without claiming anything too much for this particular poem, I think something of that happens: I think I was quite pleasurably surprised by the end.

Ken Smith

74

DEATH OF THE CAT LADY

Never liked it, this part of the city:
too damp, and the wind off the river
forever in her face, her voice
and eyes a blur trailed out
along the brickwork of the street
across the shut gate: *She's old.*
She'll not get out of bed till two.

I came a bride across the water.
I'm old. I don't belong here.
Born the other side of the river,
worked thirty years for the bank,
thirty more it seemed she'd spent
since her man, dead, willed his mother
in all her sulky humours to look after.

What she cared for were the cats
at this end of the neighbourhood
that's vaguely one way Wapping,
one way Winter Road. She knew
their names, addresses, geneologies,
moods, diets, habits, found homes
for strays, took in the homeless,
nursing gossip, mother, cats,
resentment, in her folded arms
through summer, autumn, spring.

She's dead. The neighbours
came collecting for a wreath
for Margaret at 59, our lady
of the pussycats who died
two days after mother died,
on Thursday, in the afternoon.

INTERVIEW/KEN SMITH

Are these real neighbours, people you know?

Yes, Margaret was a definite neighbour. I knew Margaret insofar as I know any of my neighbours. She lived a lot of her life at the front gate, arms folded over the gate, looking up and down the street. We called her the cat lady. I actually only knew when she was dead that her name was Margaret. Before that I just knew her as the cat lady. She looked after all the cats in the neighbourhood, and I think acted as a very essential part of the glue of a neighbourhood, of a community. Through the gossip she used to retail through the cats, she would actually be telling you what gossip she had of the neighbourhood. Quite a nice lady—I missed her when she was dead. My poem was a sort of elegy for the cat lady, for Margaret.

There's one word which seems to go deeper than the general picture of this woman. That's the word "resentment"—it suddenly comes in out of the blue: "nursing gossip, mother, cats,/resentment"—nursing resentment. What was this resentment?

The fact that she'd been looking after her mother-in-law for 30 years was one, and her man was dead, her husband was dead. So that instead of a marriage she got this family relationship when it wasn't in fact her own mother. And what she chiefly said, what she chiefly complained about, I don't belong here, I belong to the other side of the river. If you live in London, I think there's always this loyalty to north or south of the river, and she's loyal to the south of the river but lives to the north of the river. Thirty years later there she still is, where she dies, still saying 'I don't belong here'. It was as if she was somehow living the wrong life.

How did the poem actually take shape? What came first?

I think what I had in my head to begin with was the bits of it that are her voice. Particularly "I came a bride across the water", and I have a feeling that if she didn't say that, she said it in my head. That was basically what she said.

In the first stanza you don't get a great deal of help as to who is actually the subject—who is she?—"She's old./She'll not get out of bed till two".

That's the mother-in-law, whom she looks after. I realised that's actually not very clear. I make assumptions that I know I shouldn't make. If I underline something I know that's italics when it's printed and it's speech when you say it. So that when I read it I tried to change the accent in order to identify that this is Margaret talking about her mother-in-law, but I realised that it would be equally possible for it to be somebody else talking about Margaret. It's speech, but it doesn't say whose speech. So that if I were to go over it, I think I would add one word, and I'd say in the fourth line of that speech "I'm old myself" in order to identify that she's talking about someone else, this is her speech.

How would the neighbours view your description of her as being "our lady/of the pussycats"? There's a tongue-in-cheek, mocking tone there.

It's a bit mocking, and it probably sounds like what it's not meant to be—it's not actually meant to mock the Catholics or the Christians or anything like that. It was just the way I felt about it, "pussycat" being the sort of sentimental word for a cat. I did actually think of her as "our lady of the pussycats", almost like an icon. If I were a painter, I would paint her on her front porch, with her arms spread across the front of the gate and the cats all round her. I think probably in some ways I'm a frustrated painter. I wanted this icon of our lady of the pussycats, but really meant in great respect.

GLOSSARY
"humours" (line 14): moods.
"at 59" (line 27): this refers to the number of her house, not her age.

•

77

photo by Andrew Douglas

Adam Thorpe

NEIGHBOURS

My mother noticed it first, that smell
the day before her yearly garden
barbecue; lemon soufflés
in the fridge, the wobble of trifle.
For days before she'd scanned the skies
as July wilted the dahlias, steamed
in the field left fallow behind.

The stench grew serious; by dusk
we had our fists to mouths, wondered
if the blue, rather beautiful ribbons
rippling in the thistles at the back
had anything to do with it.
We strolled to the wire of the garden,
saw through the draped convolvulus

the intimate colours of our neighbours'
displayed on the field; the loud
ecstasy of flies above
that glittering clarity: the tissue
scrolled amongst thistles, small gules
of cotton-wool, the fesse of the organic.
We stumbled back and my mother

spat, feeling her health go. Me
and my father trooped round in a column;
they yelled back about a blockage
in the septic tank, and brimming bowls.
It failed to rain, but the wind
veered somewhat, towards the wood.

When they came we told each not
to look beyond the wire. One
by one, in the middle of some bright
conversation, balancing their wine
on a plate of sausages and steak,
they'd glance, quickly, then turn their heads back,
the smile still frozen on their mouths.

INTERVIEW/ADAM THORPE

Can you first of all tell me about the neighbourhood in which you live?

This is actually not where I live now, it's where I lived when I was living with my parents. This incident happened 10 or 12 years ago now. It was when I was on vacation from university. They live outside Newbury, in a hamlet, in a very ordinary modern house with a small garden, and these neighbours in fact have now moved, but it was an incident that went down in family history.

Was it the incident itself that stimulated the writing of the poem? Or was it the thought of neighbours in general and then your mind homed in on this particular one?

Yes, when I was commissioned to write the poem with the title 'Neighbours' or on the theme of neighbours, this incident actually flashed into my mind very quickly, as a very good example of a kind of overflow, a literal overflow, of one set of neighbours overflowing into the territory of another. Looking back on it we found it very funny.

When did you know the poem was finished?

Well, I was very pleased with the last line. I didn't quite know what direction it was going in, and then I got "they'd glance, quickly, then turn their heads back,/the smile still frozen on their mouths" and I thought, right, that's it. A lot of the poem is about politeness and the breaking of politeness, because we have to be polite to our neighbours if we're to get on with them. That last image, I think, of frozen politeness, that for me was the full stop.

In the second stanza, what are the "ribbons"?

That's the lavatory paper. It's our view of it. It was rather beautiful, this blue tissue, rather like the advertisements, because we were at some distance from it and couldn't quite see what it was, and of course it never occurred to us that it could be anything so unpleasant as the contents of our neighbours' septic tank.

The word "colours" in the third stanza covers a multitude of ambiguities.

The primary meaning is as in a flag or an ensign or a standard. The whole stanza is really ironic, it's looking upon it like the Wars of the Roses—I mean "gules" and "fesse" are colours and patterns on a coat of arms.

80

And "scrolled" as well picks that up.

Yes, it's like the neighbours have invaded with their colours. It's a sort of mock Wars of the Roses.

And this image moves into the fourth stanza with "Me/and my father trooped round in a column".

That's right. I feel that neighbours' fights over territory and that sort of thing, on a bigger scale can be tragic. I mean, the Wars of the Roses were families, neighbours, fighting over territory—family feuds.

The "brimming bowls", for the foreign listener, the bowls, of course, are not the bowls in the kitchen but the—

Lavatory bowls, that's right. It's all very euphemistic. "Septic tank" is, I suppose, another euphemism.

Then, finally, who does the "they" in "When they came" refer to?

The guests, not the neighbours. I had a bit of a problem there with the subject of "they", because I've said "they yelled back about a blockage/ in the septic tank"—those are the neighbours—and the "they" in the final stanza are the guests coming round.

GLOSSARY
"fallow" (line 7): uncultivated—just grass, no crops.
"convolvulus" (line 14): a weed with beautiful velvet, bell-like flowers.

81

Hugo Williams

NEIGHBOURS

The stunted sycamores put out fresh
branches to the sun. The window-cleaner's ladder
moves from house to house.
I remember drawing back the curtains
and seeing my neighbour Georgie Windows
for the first time. He was standing on the window sill
polishing the air of the open window
in 4/4 time and trying to look in. I didn't realise then
that he was the happy genius of our street,
who kept us happy and in love.
He worked at first floor level. While his old wife
went along knocking on front doors, Mr Windows
made himself known to the people upstairs
in bed. He'd been wondering, he said,
whether there was anyone living here any more
or whether we were hibernating.
He used to take his motorbike to Wales
at about this time of year. We knew it was Spring
when Georgie swore in Welsh and took off into the blue,
his eternal wife strapped to his back,
his ladder to heaven. He came home early this time
last year, having left her alone there.
He'd ridden all night and made it home in record time
just in time to go to work. She was waiting on
the doorstop for him, the house all clean and
welcoming, his favourite daffodils in every room.

INTERVIEW/HUGO WILLIAMS

When you were asked to write about the theme of "neighbours", how did you begin? What made it take this direction?

I found it quite difficult to write about neighbours without writing a personal poem. I can't really write about other people very well. I need to say "I" and "we" and think about my own relationship, and this poem is only marginally about neighbours, in that it's using a neighbour to say something about my own life. It is a little story, but it also means the coming and going of love, I suppose.

To go back to the start of the poem, how did this poem begin?

I think this one came from something Georgie must have told us, that he'd been to Wales and he'd had a row with his wife, had come back on the bike, and there she was waiting for him when he got back. She must have taken an express train and got back there before him, and it was a terrific surprise to find her standing on the pavement welcoming him, with everything clean and tidy. Or perhaps it was my imagination that she'd tidied up for him.

And that was the end of the argument?

I think so! I think she probably raced back like that to teach him a lesson, to show that she could get back just as quick without him, without his motorbike.

When did you remember noticing Georgie Windows, your neighbour, for the first time—was this a long time ago?

This was really early on, when we first moved into the street, in 1966, and Georgie had a way of getting new custom by simply going and cleaning people's windows. He was making a joke of cleaning a completely open window to make us laugh. Of course, it worked; he used to drum up custom rather early in the morning as well.

In "4/4 time"?

4/4 time is a joke about conducting. If you move your arm around the square of a window, you're cleaning it like a conductor would, in waltz time.

84

"Mr Windows/made himself known to the people upstairs/in bed" . . . *Nice play on words there.*

Well, he's a spirit of physical love, really. He makes himself known to people upstairs in bed—he's like Mr Punch, knocking on the windows and saying, 'You've got time before you go to work.' You hear the ladder clonk down on the window-sill, and there he'd be, this randy old face in the window.

Could you explain "We knew it was Spring/when Georgie swore in Welsh" and from then on?

Well, this is where the story starts really. Georgie was a Welsh Londoner; he'd get nostalgic for his home, and perhaps it's imaginary to think that his swearing in Welsh and wanting to go back to Aberystwyth was anything to do with the actual arrival of Spring, but since I'm Welsh and I sometimes yearn for roots, although my roots aren't really in Wales, I identify with him.

Then he comes home early, having left her alone. That could be interpreted in all sorts of different ways, couldn't it?

I sort of feel that he died, really, in Wales, and that she's waiting there for the funeral car to come to her door. That's why the place is so clean and welcoming—for the wake.

Yes, I confess I didn't see it that way when I read it the first time.

Well, I can't make it be there if it's not. In fact, it's there and not there, depending on who's reading it.

GLOSSARY
"stunted" (line 1): the trees have been pollarded—cut back

Kit Wright

NEIGHBOURS

I first noticed the neighbours were getting smaller
When driving away, he had to stand
To put his foot on the clutch.
She leant on tiptoe,
Getting the rubbish into the garbage bin.

That evening, returning from work,
He set his shoulder to his briefcase,
Scraping it up the garden path
And reached to the heavens with his house-key.

Later we heard through the kitchen wall
Their quarrels like kittens mewing for milk.

Later we heard through the bedroom wall
Their tiny cries of love like cries for help.

Soon we'd be putting out birdseed for them:
But who was I to intervene?
For I was growing longer, day by night.

When I shaved
In the nude
In the morning,
The mirror reflected the wrong hair.
Soon I slept with my head up the chimney,
Feet out the window,
And outfaced the treetops, tip to tip.

And when it changed and I grew lower,
My chin on the basin, chest at the toilet top,
And my voice grew slower and weaker
And lesser as their's grew louder
In sudden authority with their new-found height,

I prayed they would do me no harm
As I had done them no harm,
Nor tread on a neighbour in or out of sight.

INTERVIEW/KIT WRIGHT

It does seem to me that your poem is about tolerance, about tolerating other people or other forms of existence.

Yes indeed. It's one of those curious poems, the only one I think I've ever written, when I really don't have a very sure idea of what it's about, why I wrote it, why I came to write it, or its significance. But I do think perhaps I have in mind a metaphor of worldwide tolerance, socialistic tolerance.

I'm fairly familiar with many of your poems, and this seems to me unusually relaxed and free in its form, compared with many of your poems, which are very often written in fairly prescribed metres, and very often using rhyme.

It ends with a rhyme, it's got a few rhymes in it, but very few. I wanted to use a freer, more conversational style. I was also conscious of the fact that, among other things, the poem was going to go to an audience across the sea, was going to a foreign audience. I wanted to use the discipline of writing in a rather restricted vocabulary, if you like, or certainly a very available one, where there was nothing in it that really would need any explaining to anyone. In a way, rather like writing Esperanto. It seems to me it would be perfectly possible to write a poem in Esperanto, but you'd have to almost certainly make it a poem of ideas, rather than verbal resonances.

Yes, I can see you're perhaps less interested in the resonances or the music of the language here, than very frequently you are in other poems. On the other hand there are some, to me, very sharp and witty visual images. I suppose, in a sense, the central theme or image in this poem, is that of physical stature, and perhaps I should mention for the benefit of listeners that Kit Wright is 6' 7", not a small man at all. So how much does this effect your writing, your being unusually tall?

Not at all is the real answer to that. I have written about being tall before. I'm the sort of person who finds it very difficult sometimes to write about anything serious unless I can make a joke. And it is a fairly joky poem. I don't feel superior because I'm 6' 7"—if anything, the opposite. I think that slight inferiority complexes go with people of my sort of height. The idea was something to do with vulnerability, and I was using height, really, as a methphor there. I also think people look different to each other every day. Sometimes we appear quite different from day to day to each other. I don't mean that we literally are one day 2' high and the other day 10' tall or something, but that we do seem different to each other, and that we must learn to cope with the various moods and situations that we find ourselves in. Not only do other people look different, but we ourselves, to ourselves, look different from time to time, according to mood and so on.

AN ENORMOUS YES
in memoriam Philip Larkin
(1922–1985)

New Poems by

Harry Chambers
Robert Hull
R. A. Maitre
Andrew Motion
Meg Peacocke
William Scammell
Vernon Scannell
David Sutton
Anthony Thwaite

PHILIP LARKIN
Two unpublished poems
Two uncollected poems
'Not The Place's Fault'
(Philip Larkin writes about his Coventry childhood)
Philip Larkin on poetry
Philip Larkin on death
Photographs

and other items from the University of Hull Larkin Exhibition

Tributes by

Peter Levi · Craig Raine · David Selzer

ISBN 0 905291 85 9   PETERLOO POETS   72 pages paperback

£4.50

2 KELLY GARDENS · CALSTOCK · CORNWALL PL18 9SA

PETERLOO
POETS

NEW TITLES 1988/89
STOCKLIST
BOOKS IN PRINT & FORTHCOMING
PETERLOO POETRY CASSETTES
ASSOCIATE MEMBERSHIP SCHEME

available (*post free*) from
2 KELLY GARDENS · CALSTOCK · CORNWALL PL18 9SA

WITH THE ASSISTANCE OF

SOUTH WEST ARTS

PETERLOO POETS

"... a series kept up to scratch for a good few years by publisher Harry Chambers's energy and discrimination."
Roy Fuller/Spectator (30.1.88)

"From time to time it has seemed to me that the *Peterloo Poets* series is a haven of poetic sanity in a world of modish obfuscation."
Michael Glover/British Book News

"Harry Chambers, the publisher of *Peterloo Poets*, continues to put to shame the London publishing houses, in the flow of attractively produced volumes coming from his press. The poet who finds his major outlet in the *Peterloo* series is fortunate indeed."
D. M. Thomas/Arts South West

"I share with others an admiration for the *Peterloo Poets* imprint, particularly the way they can put the fashionable to shame and produce winners from unlikely stables."
Brian Jones/London Magazine

"*Peterloo Poets* is a small publishing house run by Harry Chambers in Cornwall. Its books are sensitively designed; each has a striking illustrated cover and the typography is excellent. The quality of production is much better than the usual standard of poetry paperbacks issued by major publishers."
G. B. H. Wightman/British Book News

"There's a solid consistency about the *Peterloo Poets* series ... Design and printing are always excellent, and the poems themselves are never less than interesting, not least because they tend to be by people who've already done some living and have something to say."
Grevel Lindop/The Times Literary Supplement

PETERLOO POETS

2 Kelly Gardens · Calstock · Cornwall PL18 9SA

CAUSLEY AT 70

(in honour of Charles Causley's 70th birthday)

Edited by Harry Chambers

Poems by

Alan Brownjohn ● Seamus Heaney ● John Heath-Stubbs
Ted Hughes ● Elizabeth Jennings ● Philip Larkin
Peter Levi ● Bill Manhire ● Roger McGough
Roger Pringle ● Lawrence Sail ● Anthony Thwaite
Chris Wallace-Crabbe ● David Wright ● Fay Zwicky

Prose Tributes by

Stanley Cook ● Dana Gioia ● Norman Levine
Edward Levy ● Colin MacInnes ● Barry Newport
Ronald Tamplin ● D. M. Thomas ● J. C. Trewin

CHARLES CAUSLEY

New poems
Uncollected autobiographical prose
Manuscript worksheets
Photographs & a selective bibliography

ISBN 0-905291-89-1

PETERLOO POETS
ISBN 0 905291 89 1
£4.95 *120 pages paperback*

00495

9 780905 291895

2 KELLY GARDENS · CALSTOCK · CORNWALL PL18 9SA